if his name is

a book in the Bible,

watch out, sis!

Delle Marianette Erracho

*to the girl who suffers quietly on her own,
I give you my voice*

*to the girl who is afraid to speak out about her experiences,
I'll stand up and pave the way*

IF HIS NAME IS A BOOK IN THE BIBLE, WATCH OUT, SIS!

Copyright © 2022 by Delle Marianette Erracho

All rights reserved. No part of this book may be used or reproduced in any form or by any means without written permission from the author except in the case of reprints in the context of reviews.

ISBN: 978-0-578-39522-7

Illustrations by Abigail Marie Perez
Book Cover by Delle Marianette Erracho
Proofread by ERA

New Edition – September 2022

Disclaimer: This book contains some words of profanity and is not at all holy like the Bible, nor is it forcing any form of religion into anyone.

PROLOGUE

Don't get me wrong, sis. Not all men with names that are in the Bible are bad. It's just self-awareness and precaution for next time.

This book is a collection of poetry and prose about my experiences in attempting to find love in the wrong places and not on God's timing. This is me facing all my demons, going through the process of healing my pain and trauma, choosing self-love and putting God first again in my life. *Everything you need to know is written between the lines.* Although most of this book is addressing certain people, these poems are messages from my heart that I wish to share with you.

I want to give affirmation to people who are hurting because of the experiences that they aren't able to share with anyone else. I want you to know that you are not alone. I have gained the courage to find my voice by turning all my emotions into poems. Writing and self-publishing this book has helped me heal. And I hope by reading it, you can find some healing, validation, and empowerment as well.

You are holding a part of my soul in your hands...

this is for all the broken hearts...

— K&K

Testaments

book of   9

book of luke   81

book of matthew & john   93

book of good and evil   107

Book of

To the guy who thought he could break me...

I saw the red flags right from the start
But I still decided to give you a chance
I let you in, thinking you'd do the same for me

I willingly gave you my time and attention
You welcomed the love I gave you
Though you were never planning on loving me back
All you did was *love bombing*

I tried to connect with you emotionally
And let myself be vulnerable with you
But when I did, you didn't even say a word
That became the first time I cried because of you

I thought I liked you
So I gave you more chances
Wishing I was mistaken about you
Turns out, it was only wishful thinking

I hoped that you would be the one
But you were never even close enough
I even asked God to give me a sign
And I got my answer when He showed me the real you

The only thing you gave me was lust
Which also came with confusion and self-doubt
But that's all you wanted from me
And that's the only thing I could hold onto

I'm not ashamed or embarrassed
For trying to get clarity and peace
When I came back to talk to you
But I was disappointed with your words

I tried my best to do right by you
And I wanted to give you my all
In the end, I'm left empty and numb

No matter how much pain and heartache you gave me
I still wanted to remember you as the person that hurt me
To help me grow and learn from these experiences

I told you I'll write a movie and dedicate it to you one day
While secretly already writing all these poems
And hoping you'd stumble upon my Instagram page

I don't have to prove to you that you were wrong
You will just see it and realize it someday
But by then, I would have moved on

I can't wish you the best
But I can pray for you to become a better person
I can't rest well at night with the thought of another girl
Falling for your lies and empty promises like I did
I just hope she will be as smart as me
To run away before it became too late

D. M. E.

my friends had a weird feeling about you
my gut told me to stay away from you
i should have listened earlier
so i didn't have to suffer

D. M. E.

Hand cover my mouth
Just enough, so I can breathe
I look up to your eyes
Your heart, I want to see

Just a touch of your finger
Makes me shiver
Your kisses linger
I want it all over

As you get closer to me
You hear, my heart's sound
As you set free
I realize, to you I'm bound

D. M. E.

i mistook the bad feeling in my stomach
as butterflies…

D. M. E.

Many came into my life but
As someone who has kept her heart protected
Never did I say yes to them
I had hoped, dreamed and
Prayed all this time for a man who would
Understand my every quirk and
Love all my flaws and inner beauty
A man who will care and give as much as I do
Then you came along and I thought I could finally
Open up my heart but it was too late before I
Realized who and what you really are

— acrostic

D. M. E.

all it took for me

to see

who you

really are

is

a broken heart

D. M. E.

Teacher,

        what i wanted was for you to *teach* me how to love

Taught

        instead you *taugh*t me how to feel hatred
        and doubt towards myself

Learn

        i had to *learn* how to accept myself through
        the bad days

Learned

        and i *learned* that you aren't good enough
        even on the good days

Lose

        i thought i'd be scared to *lose* you

Lost

        but when i *lost* you, that's when I realized...
        I'd rather lose you than lose myself to you

D. M. E.

who hurt you?
was it that bad that you couldn't let me in?
i just wanted to give you love
the kind that you deserve
even after you broke my heart
so many times

D. M. E.

Feet dangling off the bed
Sitting on top of the covers
Fingers intertwined
Arm over shoulders

Staring at your face
Watching how your lips move
Fluttering lashes as you blink

What could have been sweet moments we shared
What could have been great memories of you
What could have been a dream come true
Turned out to be my worst nightmare
One that will haunt me forever

D. M. E.

my favorite love songs
became sweeter
when you came into my life
now you're gone
i can't bring myself to listen to them
in fear that
you've spoiled them sour

D. M. E.

you've belittled me
by adoring my weaknesses
and feeding off my vulnerability

D. M. E.

When I met you, you were nothing
Then with my creative yet deceitful mind
I painted a new vision of you
How I wanted you to be
How I wished you would be for me
Then I decided to live in this world I drew in my head
Where all the scenarios are made up
And everything is sugar-coated
But like all fairytales
The princess eventually had to wake up from her daydream
And when I did
All I saw were the bad and ugly I tried to ignore
All I felt was the disappointment I wasn't expecting
All I knew was the sadness in my heart
All because I let my creativity run wild

D. M. E.

i look for you everywhere i go
i'm consistently worried
that i'd run into you
because i don't know what i'll do
and what i'd say
or worse
i don't know what you'll do
and what you'd say
that could put me back on my knees
and at your feet again

D. M. E.

i went two months without playing our favorite video game cause it reminded me too much of you. then i remembered that one time i told a guy who liked me how much i love that game. so he got it and learned how it works so we can play together. it reminded me that yeah, i'm that *type of girl.*

D. M. E.

i was holding onto the idea that maybe if i gave you enough attention, you would eventually care about me. but a time came when i got tired of giving without getting anything in return. and that's when i knew it was time to let go of the *idea of you*.

D. M. E.

Flowers

Candlelight dinners

Just a few things you promised me

What I got instead

Sore knees

Bruised ego

D. M. E.

i don't wanna cry through my makeup
it will ruin the face you once called *pretty*

D. M. E.

maybe i just liked the thought of me next to you
maybe i was intrigued by the idea that someone like you
was so interested in someone like me
maybe i was just attracted to what i saw on the outside
without knowing the awful person hidden inside
maybe i just wanted to live in a lie
even just for awhile
i should have known that this fantasy
would turn into a travesty

D. M. E.

you brought out so many things inside of me
and i tried to make sense of it all at once
i only became overwhelmed
but as i stopped to get to know myself
and to look at the depth of my wounds
i realized that it was more about me hurting inside
than you hurting me from the inside out

D. M. E.

you knew how to lure me in
to you i looked like the perfect *prey*
you locked in your target the moment you saw me
and you planned your attack as quickly as you can
when you saw my sweetness and innocence
you found a potential in me
to be conditioned to please you
anytime at your own convenience

you started with your suggestive words
and alluring messages of good night and good morning
with the red heart emojis at the end
once you learned how to play with my heart
and mess with my head
you knew i would do anything you want
including satisfying a *crave* you have

at the sound of your command
i found myself obeying your orders
as i was on my way to your house
i heard this *voice* inside
telling me to retreat and turn around
and it only kept getting louder and louder
as i was walking inside your room
i should have followed the right direction

you needed to dominate me to fulfill your hunger
but this meek lamb couldn't grasp the encounter
distracted and confused by the loud growling in my ear
i tried screaming for my voice to come back and save me
but you were the one who took it away
and that's when the prey lost to its *predator*

D. M. E.

what you thought was
just heat of the moment
burned me for life

D. M. E.

you asked me for permission
until you didn't

D. M. E.

Warning signs, warning signs
How did we show it?
Warning signs, warning signs
How did we miss it?

If you asked
How will you hear a yes or a no?
If you looked
In my body language, you'll find the answer
If you touched
You'll feel the discomfort jumping out of my skin

If I stopped
Freeze would feel like a natural response
If I looked
I would realize what I saw wasn't right
If I listened
I would hear the siren alerting me to get out

Warning signs, warning signs
Why, we sensed it was coming
Warning signs, warning signs
Why did we choose to ignore it?

D. M. E.

i've never felt more invisible
than when i was with you
i thought doing what you liked
would make you see me
when i looked at you
you weren't looking at me
you were too busy admiring
the bandage you put on me

D. M. E.

it was torture making plans that you kept turning down
it was torture when i could only see you when you wanted
it was torture every time you looked at me
with those hazel eyes but say nothing
it was torture when i felt like i couldn't say no
it was torture when i couldn't move or make a sound
it was torture every time you left me alone by myself
after you got what you wanted
it was torture when i realized that you were just using me
it was torture when i felt all that affection for nothing

interesting how the word *torture* bothered you
imagine how tortured and bothered i was

D. M. E.

you thought you could silence my mouth
little did you know...
my mind speaks louder

D. M. E.

When I beg for God's forgiveness
I'm down on both knees
I only kneel to pray
But you wanted me down to praise

Now I'm disturbed by your needs
I shouldn't have let you take the lead
If I could change anything that day
I should have got up and walked away

D. M. E.

how could i have known
that the face i used to admire
would be the same face of my perpetrator

D. M. E.

even if you deny it
it is still what happened
even if you admit it
it still doesn't make it right
even if you apologize
it still doesn't undo it
even if i forgive you
i still can't forget it

D. M. E.

i really wish you would have just asked me
before you made a move
because i would have
given you an answer

— consent

D. M. E.

it sucks
it really sucks
it really fucking sucks

D. M. E.

nothing can replace
the scent i left on your bed
the same way
i still feel that adhesive on my face

D. M. E.

i was the one who broke it off and left
but why was i the one left broken

D. M. E.

i still wonder if you really just misunderstood
or if you took advantage on purpose
i don't know which one is worse...

D. M. E.

if only they know exactly what you did to me
maybe they would understand how traumatic
that experience was that triggered me
and they won't tell me that i'm being overly dramatic

maybe instead of shaming me
they would console me
and try to understand me
if only they knew the trauma you caused me

D. M. E.

you say you don't know
you say you didn't mean to
but you knew what you were doing
and you meant to let me get hurt

D. M. E.

in your sick and twisted mind,

you like to spin my words to make it seem
like i was the crazy one
you forced me to do what you wanted
then blamed me for giving in
you accused me of miscommunication
when you were the one who didn't reply

tell me, what's it like living inside that messed up head?

D. M. E.

you were the forbidden fruit
in the tree of life
i almost took a bite
but it was rotten inside

— bad apple

D. M. E.

don't tell me what you think i'm not ready for
when you were the one who rushed me
I am ready
but no one could have prepared
for what you did to me

D. M. E.

don't accuse me of anything you don't know about me

D. M. E.

I don't burn houses, I burn bridges

D. M. E.

The same spark that lit our chemistry

Combusted into flames

Burning me from the inside like a house fire

It trapped me in the smoke and mirrors of your flattery

And your unfaltering gaslighting

But I've now come out of the fog

From the inferno you put me through

Fuming with anger

And bursting with fiery passion

I'm like a wildfire

Unstoppable, spreading uncontrollably

You will regret what you ignited in me

As you watch the embers behind

From the unexpected backfire

And the hell you've unleashed

D. M. E.

how dare you tell me what you think is best for me
when you didn't even bother to get to know me?

— fuck off

D. M. E.

i told you the first time
i don't want to be friends
yet you kept suggesting it
as if i didn't already delete
your number from my phone

D. M. E.

i didn't come knocking at your door
so you can tell me to come back
i just needed to see
if the person i was crying about
even worth it
turns out i was just wasting my time
like you wasted mine

D. M. E.

i have this constant fear that you will do to other girls what you did to me. i used to lie awake at night, crying about what happened to me…

now i cry for the girl after me

D. M. E.

if i had stayed
i don't think what we had would ever turn into love
if anything, it would have been *control*
you would have suffocated me
killing me and my spirit
but you would've enjoyed every second of it
and that's what scared me enough to leave

D. M. E.

Release me
From your hollow promises
Your deceiving words
And cunning looks

I still cry at night
Over knowing you weren't good for me
While wondering if you were ever going to be good to me

I'm tired
Of sleeping late every night
'Cause thoughts of you won't let me rest
To the point where waking up with swollen eyes
Became natural for my body

I can't feel
All the love and energy around
From the people who actually cares for me
Seeing your face in my head
Only brings me down

Not from the love you never gave me
But from your lust
And the hold you have of me

Please release me

D. M. E.

my therapist called you a narcissist
she asked me if i knew why i felt so attracted to you
she said it's because i might be a masochist
that could explain why it's hard for me to let go
because pain is all i know
and pain is all you ever gave me

D. M. E.

I keep trying to rewrite our story in my head
To explain and justify your actions
Rewinding the scenes
Coming up with different scenarios
Changing up the sequences
And replaying how the plot unfolded
Hoping you'd come out as a good character
And a love interest
To my protagonist
But when I concluded that
I was the *final girl*
And you were the scary creep I must escape
The plot twist is revealed
The story we've written
All along was a horror film
The kind you told me you like
So we were doomed right from the beginning
We could both come out alive
But in the middle
Blood and tears would have to be shed
And no one expects a happy ending

D. M. E.

like waking up from a perfect dream
you were too good to be true

D. M. E.

it's weird
i used
to like
many things
about you
but i can't
remember
anything
good

D. M. E.

i was a force of nature
you were a freak of nature
funny how as natural as it felt for us to come together
falling apart easily became natural as well

— our human nature

D. M. E.

For what felt like the longest time
I was confused and in denial
I romanticized what happened
So I wouldn't feel like a victim

I still don't think you understand
The magnitude effect of your actions
The heartache it caused me
How it cost any potential we had for a relationship

I can't go back to you now
I shouldn't
Not anymore
And never again

If you ever come across these words
I hope you take away two things
You'll never see yourself the same way again
And I will always see you in that way from now on

D. M. E.

that *fire* inside of me is back
I thought I lost it
when you almost choked all the air out of me

D. M. E.

it's crazy how we've grown up in the same town
and never crossed paths
but when we did
sadly it was so
we could break each other's hearts

D. M. E.

we could have gone our whole lives without ever meeting each other, not knowing if the other person even existed. the first time i met you, i wondered why God has never presented you to me. how did we keep on missing each other when we could have been in the same room at the same time at multiple occasions. how come i've never turned around at the moment when you could have been standing just right there. but now i know the reason... you were never meant to be part of my life at all. i was never meant to take matters into my own hands by browsing in the apps and finding my own way to you. i felt like i was punished for meeting you by mistake. so God made you a lesson that i had to learn. you were by far my most painful regret. if only i had been patient and waited for His right timing instead.

D. M. E.

I look forward to the day
When my heart stops hurting for you
When my eyes can't even shed a tear for you
When my body forgets the feeling of your touch
When my mind doesn't wonder about you at all

It will come...

D. M. E.

I tried to cut all my ties to you. But after looking for the scissors to cut you out of my life, I realized that there was a much longer cord that I haven't seen in a while. I had almost forgotten about it. Actually, I tried to live my life without ever touching that cord because it can be traced all the way back to my childhood nightmares. And it made it so much harder for me to let you go because you managed to intertwine yourself into that older cord. For quite a while, I stared at those two cords not knowing what to do about them. I thought, "Should I try to untangle one from the other? Or should I just grab my scissors and make a clean cut of the two?". Then I realized cutting you and this other cord will hurt a lot. I was terrified that I might not even survive that kind of pain when I realized that the older cord has been a part of what gives me power and strength. You just added enough weight and ate up enough energy for me to take notice of that cord again. But that was enough for me to realize that this whole time, the older cord has been the source of my purpose. I couldn't just cut it and let it go. It's become such a part of me that I can never untangle myself from it. But it also meant that you'll always be a part of that cord too. I thought to myself that I just needed to stop giving you my energy and take back my power. Take everything back that was mine before you came because I deserve all that power and energy for myself. So I decided to find your source and unplug you instead.

D. M. E.

the day i told myself
that it's really over
between us
was the day
i set myself free
from your bond

D. M. E.

You missed out...

On road trips filled with laughter and singing
On bear hugs whenever we see each other
On home-cooked meals that warms the soul
On late night deep conversations in my car
On cuddling while watching a movie
On make out sessions under the stars

You could've had all that and more...

If only you didn't mistake my kindness as my weakness
If only you didn't take advantage of my innocence
If only you listened to my needs
If only you didn't take me for granted
If only you respected me from the very beginning

You wouldn't have missed out

D. M. E.

from the moment
you pointed out the tone of my skin
and asked me where i'm from
you had decided that you're above me
and somehow better than me
you never treated me as your equal
because you don't see what you are
but i did... i saw your true colors
in the way you talk about people
and how you compare yourself to them
that i think is the worst thing about you
this complex
that came with the lightness of your skin
something your kind felt entitled to
and brainwashed into you
as you were growing up
in that hood you think is better off than mine
doesn't matter where you move to
it will always stay with you
no matter how hard you try to see it
you won't be able to change it
i wouldn't be able to help you either
and i refuse to lower myself for you
because you and i are just the way we are
you were born colorless
and i was created with flying colors

— color me woke

D. M. E.

no matter how many
beautiful lies
come out of your mouth
and how many
honest poems
i write about you
we will never speak
the same language

D. M. E.

i've sewn my wounds closed
and mended my broken heart
i'm not letting you leave any scar

D. M. E.

remember me as the girl
who tried to do her best for you
despite the circumstances
who gave you another chance
even after she got hurt
who would have given you the world
without having to ask
the girl that got away
because she knew
you couldn't give her
even half of what she deserves
because deep down
you knew you would never amount
to even an inch of her being
remember me as that girl

or not
i don't give a fuck

D. M. E.

letting you go doesn't just mean saying goodbye. it's trying to forget the idea of you i created in my mind. it's giving up on my hopes that you will change for the better and find your way back to me. it's deleting our messages and the images of you on my phone and in my head. ignoring the thoughts of you that pop up every minute of my day. it's erasing the moments we stared into each other's eyes while our fingers were interlocked. it's washing off the feeling of your body on my skin. it's holding back the tears whenever a wave of sadness hits me. pretending to be okay while i'm spending time with my family even though i'm actually falling apart. lying to my friends and saying that i'm feeling better and that i'm over you. it's endless nights of crying and grieving at our losses. it's waking up and feeling the same things all over again but still hopeful that the next day will be better. it's waiting for the day when i finally feel like i've moved on. it's trying to accept the reality of what you did to me. it's looking at the lessons that were learned. it's remembering how much i love myself before i met you and never letting myself forget ever again. it's learning how much more i want in life. it's trusting that God will always have a better plan for me than what i have for myself. it's praying but patiently waiting for the time God sends me my Godly man. *letting you go means letting in the right love that I deserve.*

D. M. E.

by the end of this book
all the words I wrote about you will be just that
just words that may or may not rhyme
but still have reason
letters that make up a message
expressed by my heart
no more tears, no more sad feelings
because after this, I will have written you in my past.

Book of Luke

D. M. E.

we were on the fourth date already
where was my flowers

D. M. E.

hold my hand
touch my hair
grab me by the waist
just do something

— what were you waiting for

D. M. E.

you're a good representative of your people

— oh Canada

D. M. E.

i regret not dating the nice guy
when i had the chance
i was too caught up in wanting
passion and excitement
when what i needed was
security and respect

— what i haven't found anywhere else

D. M. E.

i would remember a random thing about you
like your laugh
the way you dress
or when you talk code
i would smile
and be grateful that
i only have good memories of you

D. M. E.

those nights we spent
talking in my hotel lobby
walking around the city
out in the cold
looking for boba
felt like simpler times
like two innocent kids
with no clue
how to play the game
waiting on each other's move
not realizing they've already lost
'cause the time was up

D. M. E.

i never got to thank you
for trying to impress me
by playing my favorite game
i was looking forward to that virtual date
sorry i told you i just wanted to be friends
in the real world

D. M. E.

i've only seen you in moonlight
i've never seen how the sun shines in your eyes
maybe then i would have seen
the spark i was looking for

D. M. E.

i can't get over how kind you were to me. you were so nice you make the rest of them look like the spawns of Satan. don't ever change that about you. the world needs more people like you.

Book of Matthew & John

D. M. E.

you only wanted a friend out of me
when you knew i was already more than that

D. M. E.

why did you find me so cool and interesting
why did we spend nights talking on the phone
why did you want to know everything about me
why did we get along so well
why didn't we end up together
why didn't we try

D. M. E.

i like how you look with glasses
but even without it
you can still see through me

D. M. E.

thanks for walking me to class
you made me feel like i was in high school again

D. M. E.

you kept talking about our date that never happened
because you never made the time

— maybe in another lifetime

D. M. E.

you said you were always excited to see me
you thanked me because you made a lot of new friends
you found a really good job because you felt motivated
you told me your life became so much better
after you met me
you didn't tell me i wouldn't be a part of it

D. M. E.

sorry i left
without a word
is that why you act like i don't exist

D. M. E.

i'm different
than i was three years ago
will you still recognize me
will you like me now
or will you miss the old me

D. M. E.

i see you checking on me online
i don't mind
because it brings me peace
although you'll never tell
i hope you're doing good as well

D. M. E.

you proved to me
that there are
true men of God
out there
i just have to keep searching

D. M. E.

in the Bible
it says
God sends His angels
to protect us
in times
we are in need of
most

thank you for being my guardian angels
in some of the darkest days of my life

Book of Good and Evil

D. M. E.

my heart has always been fragile
i just give it to the wrong people
who don't know
how to handle it

— repeating the same mistake

D. M. E.

no one could have protected me
as sad as that sounds
it is the truth

— not as a child nor as a young adult

D. M. E.

how can one recover from a wound
that keeps getting cut?

D. M. E.

i kept asking myself why it happened to me again
and why did it have to be him
i came up empty

i tried to see the way my violators think
and why they took advantage
i saw their emptiness

D. M. E.

comes and goes
in and out
throughout our lives
but never overstays
our welcome

— happiness

D. M. E.

not everything happens for a reason. and sometimes some things happen for reasons not of your own. things happen because shit happens. and shit happens because of shitty people.

D. M. E.

now i know why i stayed single for so long
it's not because i was scared of getting hurt
it's because i didn't want to be disappointed

D. M. E.

i was feeling sick
so i ran to everyone i could
to help me cure the pain
that i was battling within
i was struggling for too long
over the truth i couldn't admit
the fear and thought of it
making me look weak
just ate me up inside
but *word vomit*
eventually had to come out

D. M. E.

you tell me i need to find what makes me happy
to keep myself busy
and focus on work
while you go on trips
go to parties
move on with your life
and leave me all alone
to figure it out on my own
i've gone through something like this before
so i've learned pretty well
how to put on a fake smile
don't be surprised
if that's all you get from me

D. M. E.

how do people walk around sober
every day that i wake up
i'm drunk with sadness
and hungover from my tears

D. M. E.

from being an independent and self-sufficient woman who does everything herself because she knows she only has herself to rely on, i've turned into someone so helpless, always needing company in my misery. i used to be the person who was so willing to care for others. i'm now realizing, no one is there to care for me.

— the hardest pill to swallow

D. M. E.

you were out there floating
while i'm here spiraling
standing my ground

D. M. E.

i couldn't sleep last night
and in the weeks before
i've tried the bottle and tonic
still i can't find rest and peace
i've been on pins and needles
with or without the pills
still the world around me keeps revolving
i'm following but not moving
i just need a minute to catch up
just give me this second of sleep

— insomniac

D. M. E.

my body refuses to move
my muscles tighten up to the point where
my lungs have forgotten how to breathe
my eyes no longer sheds water
they're dry, staring blankly at my 4 walls
then all of a sudden
my knees give in
my weight hits the floor
and i'm nailed to these wooden slabs
the room starts closing in
i'm screaming for help
through my shut lips
with no one coming to my rescue
i'm slowly dying inside my 4 walls

— depression

D. M. E.

waking up everyday triggers my anxiety

D. M. E.

i'm relying on you
cover my battle scars
make up this persona
so i can face the world
hide the exhaustion from all the crying
obvious in the depths of my sunken eyes
mask this horrible secret
buried under layers of foundation
don't let them see the reason
behind this hollow emotion
i'm tired of seeing only darkness
brighten up my eyes
so i can live in the light again

— concealer

D. M. E.

when people start a sentence with
no offense
or *don't take this the wrong way*
it's like they're washing the blame
off their hands
and putting it on you instead
so it becomes your fault
if you get offended
but shouldn't they be the ones
who should feel bad
for saying something
they already know
will hurt you

D. M. E.

if his name is a book in the Bible
watch out, sis
you might think
he's an angel
sent down from the heavens
by God
but so was Lucifer

D. M. E.

the whole time i was on the chair
with a needle stabbing permanent ink into my skin
while jabbing at the bone of my finger
all my mind can think was...

Fuck you,
Fuck you,
Fuck you,

D. M. E.

something's changed in me
and i think people are starting to notice
there's a new meaning behind my sad eyes
but no one is brave enough to ask

D. M. E.

they just don't understand
they don't bother enough to care
and they don't care enough to ask

— parents

D. M. E.

true love sounds like a joke
i once heard as a kid

D. M. E.

i envy people
who have intuition
that tells them
if a person is bad
i don't know why i grew up
having so much faith
in people
when all they do
is tear me down
yet again
i am here
still hoping
for love
from people
who will always
let me down

D. M. E.

why is it so hard for someone to love me back
do i love too hard
or am i too hard to love

D. M. E.

what are you doing, sis? why are you out here waiting on people to get back to you as if your time isn't valuable? why are you doing this to yourself? *STOP!* you give so much time and attention to other people that they've stopped respecting your time and attention. i know it's just who you are and it's hard to change that. i know you can't help being yourself even though being yourself means that you're the one that ends up hurting. i understand you. trust me, i do. but sometimes you just gotta learn when to let go to do what's best for you.

D. M. E.

i'm sensitive

          NO, i'm just full of passion

i'm overreacting

          NO, I'm just overwhelmed

i'm acting crazy

          NO, you've just never seen a girl stand up for herself

i'm being ridiculous

          NO, you just can't handle the truth

D. M. E.

you know
that it wasn't your fault
but it's hard
to admit to yourself
because you're afraid
to say its name
so you just say
he took advantage

what happened to you
is the devil's work
men do to women all the time

in this battle
you're fighting
you are not alone
so when you're ready
you call that devil by its name
that's the only way to defeat it

— sexual assault

D. M. E.

i kept playing it off as a heartbreak
but i couldn't play the denial game anymore
when i was my own opponent in this losing game
i thought claiming defeat was the only move
but i learned that just by speaking my truth
it would claim me as the winner

— a game i didn't want to play

D. M. E.

people told me what it was
but i dismissed it
i couldn't wrap my head around it
i was still in shock and in denial
it took me awhile
but when i finally came to my own realization
that's only when i started healing from it

D. M. E.

i didn't realize how lost i was
until i found myself at His door
i may crawl back in tears
but His open arms
always takes away my fears

D. M. E.

i reached out my hand to her
and pulled her out of the darkness
proving to her that
she's always been the sunshine
that gives me life
and endless faith
the reason for my existence
the reason i bloom
the reason i breathe
i live for her

D. M. E.

i'm allowing myself to feel everything
all the things i've held back
in hopes of not getting hurt
but people hurt me anyway
it's better to face all the emotions now
so i can heal sooner
than to keep it all inside
and have it exploding later
into a million small pieces
that i can't recognize
a piece of myself
anymore

D. M. E.

instead of screaming out my anger to the world
i will write, sing, dance, create, and love even harder

D. M. E.

telling my story
used to feel like
breaking my heart
all over again
but telling my truth
feels like i'm
putting the broken pieces
back together

D. M. E.

no matter when and how
you decide to tell your story
i want you to know
your experience matters

D. M. E.

I believe you. I believe your story and I validate your experiences. I believe that it was not your fault and you are not the problem. I believe this situation will not hinder you from living your life to the fullest. I believe you have the capability of rising above this this trial. I believe you are so much more powerful than you could ever know. I believe you have so much more to show and share with the world. I believe that God has so many plans in store for you in this lifetime. I believe you deserve all the happiness in this whole universe. I believe you are much more than enough.

I believe in you, sis

D. M. E.

there's nothing wrong with being broken. if broken is what you feel inside, then that's what you feel and that's okay. your feelings are valid. just know that you are not stuck being broken and this moment does not define you or the rest of your life. just take your time picking yourself back up and putting your pieces back together. it takes a lot of self-love, patience, and understanding. but i know you can do it. no one else can make you feel whole again better than yourself. and you are doing a great job.

D. M. E.

no one is ever going to fully understand you, what you're feeling, what you're thinking, and what you're going through. no one else but you. so be kinder and be more forgiving to yourself. i'm sure you'll understand.

D. M. E.

yeah i know, sis. it's hard. it's hard to be yourself in a world full of cruel people. but don't stoop yourself to their level. don't let yourself turn into one of them as a way of revenge. you are perfect where you are and just being yourself is perfect. in the right time, someone will see all your efforts and take all that load off your hands. you will realize that being yourself in a world full of cruel people will be alright with someone who will always let you be yourself.

D. M. E.

read all the signs
listen to your heart
ask for advice
always think twice
before making a decision
pray and sleep on it
reach out for help
go to therapy
don't ever be afraid to say no
do everything you need to do
to protect
who should matter most
in this world
you
&
only you

D. M. E.

i'm taking it back

my voice
my body
my energy
my power
my life

i took it all back

i tried to make sense of everything that happened to me in the last year. why the new people i met easily became my friends. why some old friends became acquaintances. why people left as fast as they came. why i left in some relationships. why things turned out the way they did. why the good moments, although many, didn't last for long. and why the bad never seemed to end. what were the lessons i learned. what were the mistakes i made. what can i change for the better next time. and how can i improve my own life. i now get it, that as a human being, that's all i can really do in this world. live and learn. understand and forgive. be kind and spread love. as i looked to God for answers and His help, i found my new purpose in this world. to share my experience to all women. to give them the same support and validation that i needed during this time. and hopefully warn and educate them about the signs before it happens to them. i am no where near perfect or all-knowing. but if i can inform others and if i can save someone from sexual assault, then everything i went through would be worth something and i will have served God's purpose for me in this world.

D. M. E.

sa agos ng hangin
sa bawat patak ng ulan
sa mataas na bundok
ibabaw ng langit
at ilalim ng dagat
kahit sa init ng iyong hininga
doon mo makikita
at mararamdaman
ang Kanyang pag-ibig
na walang hanggan
at walang katumbas
lahat ay biyaya ng Diyos
para lang sa atin
oh kay gandang mabuhay
sa mundong Kanyang gawa
itong buhay ko
ay handog
para sa Kanya

D. M. E.

i've been in love before
so deeply...
with the words spoken by my passionate heart

i've given life before
so greatly...
to the ideas created by my beautiful mind

i've dealt with pain before
so devastatingly...
caused by the effect of people here and there

i've seen true beauty before
so magnificently...
in all of God's creations above and below

D. M. E.

we made it, sis
we survived
tired and a little broken
but still alive
slowly but surely
we are healing
i'm not gonna lie
every day will be a struggle
there will be moments throughout your day
when you'll feel sad, angry, or depressed
or all of those at the same time
but i know you'll get through it
like always
just remember to breathe
ground yourself to be reminded
that you are here in this present
and you are finally safe
you will always have your power and self-love
to guide you through
I'm proud of us, sis!

Thank you for reading my story. If you let me, I can be the person to hold your hand in your dark times. There were a lot of moments in my life when I felt like no one was there to hold mine when I needed the support. It's so easy to let yourself think that you are alone in your pain because people will make you feel that it's your fault and they'll make you doubt the person you know you are. But not here. I don't ever want you to feel like you're alone in your experiences. Through my poems and my story, I hope I was able to reach you in time. You may or may not know me personally, but I sincerely mean it when I say I am here if you need an ear to listen, a shoulder to cry on, and arms to give you a warm hug. Please don't hesitate to reach out to me, or to professionals. It's important that you know that your experience matters and there will always be love and acceptance here for you.

— D. M. E.

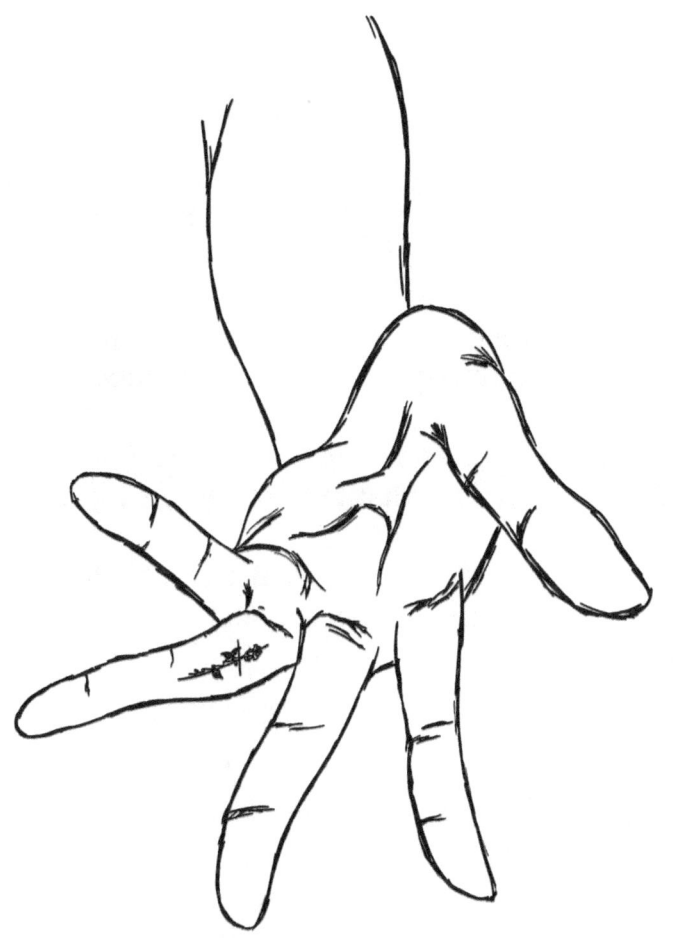

Special Thanks & Message

Catherine, my therapist
&
Kirsten, my mentor

Thank you for sharing your story with me and for empowering me to tell mine.

You helped me validate my own experience and assured me that I matter in this world.

My only hope is that I will also be able to do the same for others.

If you are someone who is afraid to talk about your sexual assault experience in fear of judgment and victim-blaming, please call the **National Sexual Assault Hotline** to get the help and advice you deserve and need like I did.

1 - 800 - 656 - 4673
Or visit **RAINN.ORG**

ABOUT THE AUTHOR

Delle Marianette Erracho is Filipina American, born in Manila, Philippines. She moved to the USA in 2006 and has lived in Vallejo, California ever since. She is a professional photographer and filmmaker, and an aspiring poet and book author. At 26 years old, Delle Marianette wrote and self-published her first short poetry collection titled, *GENESIS*, followed by her official poetry book titled, *If His Name Is A Book In The Bible, Watch Out, Sis!*. She wants to serve as an advocate and be the voice for the people who struggle dealing with their sexual assault experience and mental health.

All her creative mediums are reflections of her life story through the perspective and experiences of being a woman, POC, 1st generation immigrant, and a striving artist.

For excerpts from the book and updates about the author, follow her on Instagram:

@dellemarianette
@dmepoetry

If you live in the U.S., here are some other resources available to you. Please seek out if you need any help. Choose yourself first. Choose life.

❖ *National Suicide Prevention Lifeline*
   1 - 800 - 273 - 8255 or 9 - 8 - 8
   Or visit **suicidepreventionlifeline.org**

❖ *National Domestic Violence Hotline*
   1 - 800 - 799 - 7233
   Or visit **thehotline.org**

❖ *National Alliance on Mental Illness Helpline*
   1 - 800 - 950 - 6264
   Or visit **nami.org**

❖ *Substance Abuse and Mental Health Services Administration Helpline*
   1 - 800 - 662 - 4357
   Or visit **samhsa.gov**

❖ *Teen Line*
   1 - 800 - 852 - 8336
   1 - 310 - 855 - 4673
   Or visit **teenline.org**

There is so much hope and love out there. You deserve to live the rest of your life to find out for yourself.